TWO TICKETS TO FREEDOM

THE TRUE STORY OF
ELLEN AND WILLIAM CRAFT,
FUGITIVE SLAVES

TWO TICKETS TO FREEDOM

The True Story of Ellen and William Craft, Fugitive Slaves

FLORENCE B. FREEDMAN

ILLUSTRATED BY

Ezra Jack Keats

PETER BEDRICK BOOKS

NEW YORK

Published by Peter Bedrick Books
2112 Broadway
New York, NY 10023

Library of Congress Cataloging-in-Publication Data

Freedman, Florence B. (Florence Bernstein)
Two tickets to freedom : the true story of Ellen and William
Craft, fugitive slaves / Florence B. Freedman ; illustrated by Ezra
Jack Keats.
p. cm.
Reprint. Originally published: New York : Simon and Schuster,
1971.
Summary: Traces the search for freedom by a black man and wife who
traveled to Boston and eventually to England after their escape from
slavery in Georgia.
ISBN 0-87226-330-4.—ISBN 0-87226-221-9 (pbk.)
1. Fugitive slaves—United States—Biography—Juvenile literature.
2. Fugitive slaves—England—Biography—Juvenile literature.
3. Craft, Ellen—Juvenile literature. 4. Craft, William—Juvenile
literature. 5. Afro-Americans—Biography—Juvenile literature.
6. Slavery—United States—History—19th century—Juvenile
literature. [1. Craft, William. 2. Craft, Ellen. 3. Fugitive
slaves. 4. Afro-Americans—Biography.] I. Keats, Ezra Jack, ill.
II. Title.
E450.F8 1989
973'.0496073022—dc20
[B]
[92]   89-34109
CIP
AC

Manufactured in the United States of America
5 4 3   94 95

Contents

I

The Mysterious Traveler

Early in the morning, on Wednesday, December 21, 1848, a slim, well-dressed young man entered the station at Macon, Georgia, rushed to the ticket window, and panted, "Tickets for myself and my slave."

"Yes, sir; thank you, sir." The ticket agent quickly handed the young man the tickets and the change, for it was almost time for the train to leave. "Your seat is in the first car. Your boy will ride in the last car with the others."

The young man seemed distressed. "Can't William ride with me?" he asked in a soft, low voice. "As you can see, I am nearly helpless without him." Indeed, the young man's right arm was in a sling, his face was bandaged, and his eyes were shaded by green eyeglasses.

"It is not customary, as you know sir; other passengers would object. He can come to serve you when you need him. I wish you a pleasant and successful journey, sir."

"A-l-l a-b-o-a-r-d!" called the conductor.

Just as the train was about to start, a thickset man raced along the platform, staring frantically into each window as he passed. When the young man saw him, he drew in his breath sharply and hastily turned his head away. Before the man came to the last car, however, the train had picked up speed and was chugging on its way.

Most of the passengers were on their way to Savannah. For the young man and his slave, however, Savannah was only the first stop on a four-thousand-mile journey.

If the ticket agent had known who the two really were, instead of "Yes, sir" and "Thank you, sir" and "Have a pleasant journey, sir," he would have shouted, "Seize them! Help! Escaping slaves!"

If the thickset man running along the platform had recognized the bandaged young passenger, or had reached the last car and seen the slave William, the two travelers would have been forcibly removed from the train and dragged back to their masters.

If they had been caught, their captors, tearing the bandage from the young man's face and pulling off the green eyeglasses, would have seen the smooth cheeks and frightened eyes of a woman. For the "man" and his slave were Ellen and William Craft, both slaves from Macon, who had determined on a desperate plan to set themselves free.

The train chugged on, each turn of the wheels bringing them nearer to freedom. But the road ahead was not as smooth as the shining rails.

Only five days before they boarded the train, Ellen and William Craft had seemed to be contented slaves. Other slaves envied them. Ellen and William did not have to work long hours in the fields, as others did, nor were they shouted at or beaten by overseers. They did not have to live in broken-down cabins; they never went hungry.

Although William belonged to Mr. Ira Taylor and Ellen to Dr. and Mrs. Robert Collins, they were allowed to live together as husband and wife. Dr. Collins had given them a neat room in a cottage on his land. Ellen, who served as Mrs. Collins' personal maid, even made some of Mrs. Collins' dresses, for Ellen was a talented seamstress.

William went to work every morning, just as free workmen did. He was a skillful cabinetmaker and worked in a shop. His wages, however, went to his master, Mr. Taylor. Unlike other slaves, William sometimes had a little money of his own, for his employer permitted him to work overtime and gave him the money he earned for those hours. William was able to get little things for Ellen and himself. He bought wood out of which he made a small chest of drawers for Ellen. In it they kept the money he earned and saved. This chest of drawers proved to be most useful in the days before Christmas in the year 1848.

Compared to other slaves, Ellen and William were very fortunate—but the thought of escaping was never far from their minds. For in their childhood, both had seen the bitterness of slavery.

Ellen was born in 1826 in the household of a wealthy slaveowner who was one of the founders of the city of Macon, Georgia. Ellen's mother was one of this man's slaves. Slaves were the property of their owners, who could do whatever they wanted to with them—set them to work in the house or in the fields, feed them or starve them, punish them, sell them, or even have them killed. Sometimes a master found a slave woman attractive, and might secretly treat her as if she were his wife. But if

she bore a child, according to the law the child was a slave, following the condition of the slave mother, not that of the free father.

So it was with Ellen. Her father was her mother's owner, and Ellen, who resembled her father, was to all appearances white. But she was a slave. Her mother loved her dearly, but her master paid no more attention to her than to any other slave child, and his wife, Ellen's mistress, always treated her harshly. Although Ellen was a pretty, polite and bright child, nothing she could say or do pleased her mistress. Ellen did not realize that her very presence offended her mistress, because she was the child of her husband and a slave woman. No matter how hard little Ellen tried to be helpful—dusting while her mother cleaned house, setting the table, sewing neatly with the finest of stitches—she was sure to get scoldings, slaps, and often a box on the ear from her mistress.

When Ellen cried or complained, her mother would remind her how well off she was compared to the other slave children on the plantation. Because her mother worked in the house, Ellen always had enough to eat. (Rich folks left enough on their plates to feed a family.) Ellen knew that slaves who were not house servants often had only one meal a day, and that was likely to be just a cake made of cornmeal or a potato. Ellen's work—helping her mother—was easy. Most slave children worked from sunup to sundown in the fields with their mothers. A four-year-old child would often have to sit all day at the edge of the field taking care of a baby brother or sister, not permitted to stir from the spot. If the mother carried her baby on her back while she worked, her other children, as soon as they could walk, worked at their mother's side. Sometimes slaves worked knee-deep in water and mud in the marshy rice fields. Ellen knew that her punishments were mild compared to the floggings that women and children, as well as men, got from the overseers.

Yet Ellen wished that just once something she did would please her harsh mistress!

"Nothing matters, honey, as long as we are together," her mother would console her. "Just so you are not sold away from me!"

It was not kindness or consideration for either Ellen or her mother that had prevented Ellen's mistress from selling one or both of them years before. She knew that her husband would never have permitted it.

One day, when Ellen was eleven years old, a visitor to the house said to Ellen's mistress, "What a pretty little daughter you have!"

"She's not my daughter! She's a slave!" her mistress snapped. This was the last straw. But this time she could do something about it. Her daughter Eliza was to be married. Surely the father of the bride could not object to giving his daughter the little slave as a wedding present.

Eliza was married to Dr. Robert Collins in 1837, and eleven-year-old Ellen became the slave of Mrs. Collins. Although she was very sad at parting with her mother, Ellen was glad to leave the household of her tyrannical mistress.

Ellen's new master was a very wealthy man. As owner of the Monroe and Bibb Railroad and Banking Company, he had built the railroad from Macon to Oconee, and brought the first telegraph lines into Macon. He owned 10,000 acres of farmland and sixty-two slaves.

Ellen was taken to live on College Hill in a mansion set among trees in the midst of four acres of gardens.

The estate was opposite Wesleyan College which Dr. Collins had helped to found.

Ellen's new mistress was always kind to her, and she grew up in the beautiful house as her mistress's personal maid. But Ellen could not be happy. She missed her mother and her friends. She thought it was unfair that her old mistress had been able to give her away as a present—as if she were a *thing*, not a *person*. She could not forget the harsh lives of other slaves. She vowed she would never marry and have children, because her children could never be hers—they would always belong to her owner, and could be torn from her, just as she had been taken away from her mother. They could even be sold away from her. Ellen's life was like a candy-coated pill. Outwardly it was pleasant, but she could never forget the bitter core of slavery.

William's life as a child had been harsher than Ellen's. He was one of a large family, which meant that he had had to endure a series of tragic separations. His father and mother had had five children in slavery—three boys and two girls. Although their lives were hard, they were a loving and close-knit family, helping each other whenever they could. William's mother and father were hard-working and loyal to their master. Knowing that their master had vast cotton fields and needed lots of slaves, they did not imagine he would ever sell them or their children.

But when William's parents grew old, their master did not want the burden of having to feed and care for them. He thought it would be a good idea to sell them before they became so old that they would be worthless in the market. He thought nothing of the fact that they had been married for many years and had children—

children who, being young and strong, were worth keeping. So he sold William's mother and father at different times and to different owners. They were never to see each other again. The partings of husband and wife, and of the parents and their children, were tearful and tragic.

William and his brothers and sisters burned with rage and sorrow, but tears and sobs could not make their master change his mind, and they had to suppress their anger. They could only hope that the five of them could stay together. But that was not to be. Their master found he was short of money, so he sold one brother and one sister—again to two different owners.

There was another way, however, besides selling, in which a slave could bring his master income. If the slave was a skilled workman, he could be hired out and his owner would receive his wages. William's master therefore arranged for William and his remaining brother to learn trades. He apprenticed William to a cabinetmaker, and his brother to a blacksmith.

Before William's brother finished his apprenticeship, however, the master sold him. The master wanted to speculate in cotton (to buy cotton before it was harvested and wait, hoping that prices would go up). He tried to borrow money from a bank. The banker was willing to give him a loan, but only in the form of a mortgage: that is, the borrower had to put up something of value that the lender could take if the loan was not repaid. If someone borrows money from a pawnshop, for example, he must give the pawnbroker a watch or a ring or something else of value as security. This becomes the pawnbroker's property if the borrower does not repay the loan. Sometimes people mortgage their homes as security for a loan. Slaves, as property, could also be mortgaged, and so William's master mortgaged the sixteen-year-old William and his fourteen-year-old sister. When it was time to repay the bank, William's master didn't have the money, and the bank became the owner of the two young slaves. In order to get back its money, the bank arranged to sell William and his sister at a slave auction.

William never forgot that terrible day. Buyers came and looked the slaves over as if they were horses, feeling their muscles, examining their mouths to see if their teeth were sound, testing their strength by having them lift heavy boxes and barrels.

As each slave was put upon the auction block, the auctioneer would call, "What am I bid?"

"Fifty dollars," someone would shout.

"He's worth at least two hundred, and you know it."

"Sixty dollars."

"I bid seventy."

Men would call out offers, until at last a bid was made which no one else would top.

"Two hundred dollars once; two hundred dollars twice; two hundred dollars third and last time. Fairly warned! Sold to the gentleman from Savannah for two hundred dollars."

After several slaves had been sold, William's sister was put on the block. She stood trembling; with her eyes downcast and her arms clasped in front of her as if she was trying to shrink into herself. William was filled with pity and anger. After one look, which he meant to be encouraging, he turned his eyes away and tried to blot out the sound of the auctioneer's voice and the bids from the crowd.

Suddenly William realized that the bidding was over, that his sister was being led away by her new master. At the same time he was being prodded to mount the auction block. He knew that he would never see his sister again. He had to say goodbye to her. A friend of his, a slave who had come to the auction with his master, was standing near the block. William leaned down, and said, "Please run to my sister's new owner, and beg him to wait a few minutes until I am sold, so that I can say goodbye to my sister."

The friend raced away, but came back saying, "He won't wait. He says he has far to go and must get started."

William then dropped to his knees and begged the auctioneer to stop the bidding for just a few minutes to allow him to say goodbye to his sister. The auctioneer grabbed him by the neck and pulled him to his feet, saying, "Get up! You can do the wench no good. There's no use in your seeing her!"

From the auction block William saw his sister in the back of her master's cart, sitting with clenched hands. He could even see the tears running down her cheeks, yet he could not go to her. She bowed, as if in farewell. William fixed his eyes upon her until she vanished from sight.

The auction went on. William felt like crying, but he clenched his teeth and stood up tall. He did not hear the bidding. He moved this way and that as he was told. He flexed his muscles and lifted a heavy case on command. But he felt his brain on fire as he silently prayed for the power to rescue his sister some day.

William could not know that some good was going to come of this auction.

William was bought by Mr. Ira Taylor, an employee of the bank owned by Dr. Robert Collins, Ellen's master. As a result of the association of their owners, William and Ellen were bound to meet.

Mr. Taylor sent William back to work in the cabinet shop where he had been working. His life went on as before.

Some years later, William and Ellen met and fell in love. For several years they did not want to become husband and wife, because both remembered having been torn from their parents. Love finally prevailed and they asked for and were given permission to live together as husband and wife. (Slaves were not allowed to have religious or civil marriages, for the owners wanted to be able to separate them and sell their children if they wished to.) William and Ellen were happy together, but they determined never to have children in slavery.

And the thought of escape never left their minds.

II

~⚓~

Escape in Style

EVERY once in a while William and Ellen would hear from other slaves or workmen at the shop about slaves who had tried to get away. Ellen sometimes overheard talk among her mistress's guests about "niggers" who didn't know how well off they were and tried to run away to the North. At times she heard of the hateful "abolitionists" who lured slaves away from their good homes and their kind owners. After listening to them, Ellen thought abolitionists were fearful monsters.

When Ellen and William heard of slaves who ran away they prayed for their safety. But too many were caught. Tracked by bloodhounds and by men on horseback, the poor slaves blundered through forests, stumbled in stony streams and swam rivers to elude their pursuers. But they were usually caught and brought back. Overseers beat them until they were half-dead, as a lesson to others who might think of running away. William and Ellen heard of one slave who had himself packed in a case and shipped North. He was starving and almost suffocated when the crate was opened—but he was free.

Sometimes a man tried to escape alone, hoping that when he got up North he could work and save money to buy his wife's freedom.

William was brave enough and strong enough to have taken a chance as others did, in spite of bloodhounds and the fear of punishment. But he would not leave Ellen. He knew he had to think of a plan that would save them both.

William often thought that because Ellen could pass for white, she might escape without being caught. She looked like a white woman, and because she had always worked in the house as a personal maid, she talked the way her mistress did.

William had saved more than enough money for the journey. How wonderful it would be, he thought, if he could buy railroad tickets for himself and Ellen! But it was against the law for any public conveyance—train, stagecoach, or boat—to take slaves without their masters' consent. If they were discovered, slave hunters could snatch them from the train and drag them back—but not to the comfortable little room and to the pleasant jobs they had had. As escaped slaves they would be whipped and put to hard labor in the fields. And they might be sold to different masters, never to see each other again. Some escaped slaves had even been tortured to death as a warning to others.

How to escape? Would it be possible for Ellen to pretend she was a white lady and have William accompany her as her slave? No, that would never do, because a lady would not travel alone with a male slave; ladies took only female slaves with them on journeys.

Eight days before Christmas, 1848, William thought of a clever and daring plan. If Ellen could be disguised as a young gentleman, he could travel with her as her slave. They could go by train from Macon to Savannah, and then on to Philadelphia and freedom!

When he told Ellen of his plan, however, she was fearful. "It is too much for us to undertake," she said. She did not think that she could play the part of a free, white young gentleman for the long journey of a thousand miles until they reached a free state. But after considering the alternative—remaining in slavery, where she was just a possession, not a human being, and where her children would be possessions of the master—she finally agreed.

"God is on our side; with His assistance, we will be able to succeed." She told William to buy the disguise. "I will try to carry out the plan," she promised.

Even the purchase of the disguise was difficult. It was against the law in Georgia for a white man to trade with a slave without his master's consent. Still, there were some storekeepers who were willing to sell to slaves— not because they were sympathetic to the slaves, but because a slave could never tell on them, since a slave could not testify in court against a free white person.

William stealthily went to different parts of town at odd times, buying a coat, a shirt and a hat for Ellen, and a hat for himself. In this way he was able to acquire everything needed for Ellen's disguise, except a pair of trousers. These Ellen had to sew for herself. Ellen hid all the purchases in the chest of drawers William had made for her.

There was still one obstacle. In order to travel even a few miles from their home, Ellen needed written permission from her mistress and William from the cabinetmaker. Kindly slave owners sometimes allowed the slaves a few free days to visit family or friends at Christmas, and so Ellen asked her mistress to allow her to visit a dying old aunt twelve miles away. Mrs. Collins consented, and gave Ellen the necessary pass. William's employer reluctantly gave William a pass to permit him to accompany Ellen, but urged him to return as soon as possible, as he needed him badly. William promised to do so. Later the cabinetmaker became suspicious, and it was he who ran down the platform peering into the train windows, looking for them.

When William returned to the cottage, he showed Ellen his pass and she showed him hers. They held them as if they were treasures—but they could not read them.

They had the precious passes. But there was another difficulty. Ellen suddenly realized that travelers had to register their names in the visitors' book at hotels, as well as in the clearance book in the Custom House in South Carolina, and her spirits fell. For she could not write. Ellen had wanted to learn to read and write, and her mistress might have consented to teach her. Unfortunately, however, it was against the law to teach slaves to read and write. She and William had taught themselves to recognize and print a few letters of the alphabet, but they could not write even their names.

It looked as if William's idea of escaping with Ellen in disguise would never work.

Suddenly Ellen raised her head, smiled through her tears, and said, "I think I have it! I can make a bandage and bind up my right hand in a sling, and ask the hotel proprietors to register my name for me."

It then occurred to Ellen that the smoothness of her face might betray the fact that she was a woman. She decided to place a bandage on her cheek, and tie a scarf under her chin and over her cheeks, as if she were suffering from a bad toothache. But would not her eyes betray her fear? William went to yet another shop and bought a pair of green eyeglasses for her.

William and Ellen stayed up all night going over their plans, trying to think of all situations that might arise. Just before the time arrived for them to leave, William cut off Ellen's hair. Ellen then dressed in her disguise.

When the moment came for them to leave, William and Ellen blew out the lights and knelt in prayer, begging God to help them escape from bondage as He had helped the Israelites of old to escape from bondage in Egypt.

The decisive moment had come. Once they opened their cottage door, and Ellen stepped outside as a young gentleman, there could be no turning back.

Fearful that someone might have overheard their plans and be lurking about, William took Ellen by the hand, moved toward the door, raised the latch, and peeped out. The trees around the house were like sentinels. Not a leaf moved. Everything was as still as death.

"Come, my dear," William whispered to Ellen. Ellen hesitated, drew back, and burst into violent sobs.

After a few minutes, however, she became calm. "Come, William," she said, "I am ready."

William locked the door for the last time and put the key into his pocket, though he knew he would never use it again. Cautiously they tiptoed across the yard and into the street.

There they solemnly shook hands, said farewell, and went separately, along different streets, to the railway

station. William hurried, but Ellen went slowly, as she wanted to get to the station just before the train was due to leave.

The journey, which had really begun when Ellen and William were born into slavery, continued. They were now heading toward freedom.

III

An Eventful Trip

ELLEN CRAFT, who now called herself Mr. Johnson, seated herself near the window of the train compartment and sighed with relief. The first part of their plan had been successful. They were on the train heading North—she in a first-class carriage and William in the car with other slaves. She turned to look at her fellow passengers.

Then Ellen's heart sank. Seated right next to her was Mr. Cray, a friend of her master's who had had dinner at the Collinses' the night before, and who had known Ellen since childhood. "He has come to find me and take me back," she thought in terror.

But Mr. Cray said nothing and made no move. Evidently he was just a passenger.

But Ellen's fears persisted. She thought to herself, "Suppose he starts a conversation with me. . . . He might recognize my voice." She decided to make believe she was deaf if he should speak to her.

After a few minutes, Mr. Cray said, "It's a very fine morning, sir."

"Mr. Johnson" took no notice, but kept looking out of the window.

"It's a very fine morning, sir," repeated Mr. Cray in a louder tone.

Still no answer from "Mr. Johnson."

Other passengers began to stare. One of them laughed.

"I will make him hear!" vowed Mr. Cray, and shouted, "IT IS A VERY FINE MORNING, SIR!"

At this, "Mr. Johnson" turned his head, as if hearing him for the first time, and said only, "Yes," and turned again to the window.

"It is a very great deprivation to be deaf," commented one of the other passengers.

"Yes," answered Mr. Cray, "and I shall not trouble that fellow any more."

They had passed two crises, thought Ellen; the cabinetmaker had not found William, and Mr. Cray had not recognized her. What new crises were in store for them?

While "Mr. Johnson" remained silent, the other gentlemen in the railroad carriage whiled away the time by talking of the three favorite topics of Southern gentlemen—cotton, "niggers," and abolitionists. Ellen had always thought of abolitionists as some kind of wild animals; now she learned that they were people opposed to slavery, people who often helped slaves to escape. This was a useful piece of information. At last the gentlemen all left the carriage at Gordon, for they were bound for Milledgeville, then the capital of the state.

Early in the evening the train arrived at Savannah. "Mr. Johnson" and his slave, with the other passengers, were driven in a horse-drawn omnibus to a hotel where they were to have tea. Ellen did not leave the omnibus. William brought her a tray of food.

The omnibus took them to the steamer, which was bound for Charleston, South Carolina. Trying to avoid encounters with the other passengers, "Mr. Johnson" retired early. Ellen suggested that William prepare flannel bandages where all could see him, so as to make it clear that his master was ill. William warmed the bandages and liniment on the stove in the ship's lounge.

His activity was certainly noticed!

"Buck, what have you got there?" asked one of the passengers.

"Opodeldoc, sir," William replied. (This was the name of the liniment.)

"I should think it's opo*devil*," said another man, who was leaning back in his chair with his feet on the back of another chair, and chewing tobacco vigorously. "It stinks enough to kill or cure twenty men! Away with it, or I reckon I will throw it overboard."

William, having given evidence of the fact that his master was really sick, took the warm flannel cloths and the opodeldoc to his master, stayed a little while, as if applying the bandages, and then went back on deck.

"Where should I sleep, sir?" he asked the steward.

"We have no place for colored people, slave or free," was the answer.

William paced the deck for hours, then found a few cotton bags in a warm place near the funnel. There he sat until morning, when he went to help his "master" get ready for breakfast.

At breakfast, "Mr. Johnson" was seated at the right hand of the captain, who, together with other passengers, inquired about his health. William cut the food for his master, then went out.

"You have a very attentive boy, sir," said the captain. (It was a good thing Ellen was wearing green eyeglasses, or the captain would have seen her eyes flash fire as he referred to her husband as "boy." But that was the way in the South. A black man was called "boy" until he was old, and then he was called "uncle." Never *man*, or *sir*. Sometimes "boy" or "uncle" might be said affectionately—but the words grated nevertheless.) The captain continued, "You had better watch him like a hawk when you get to the North. He seems all very well here, but he may act quite differently there. I know several gentlemen who have lost their valuable slaves among them damned cutthroat abolitionists."

Before "Mr. Johnson" could answer, a rough slave dealer, who was sitting with his elbows on the table and a piece of chicken in his hand, mumbled through a full mouth, "Sound doctrine, Captain, very sound!"

The slave dealer dropped the chicken on the plate, put his thumbs into the armholes of his fancy waistcoat, and continued: "I would not take a slave to the North under no consideration. I have had a deal to do with slaves in my time, but I never saw one who ever had his heel upon free soil that was worth a damn!"

The slave dealer then turned to "Mr. Johnson": "Now, stranger," he said, "if you have made up your mind to sell that boy, I am your man. Just mention your price and if it isn't out of the way, I will pay for him on this board with hard silver dollars."

Staring at Ellen as the serpent did at Eve, the slave dealer went on. "What do you say, stranger?"

"I don't wish to sell, sir," replied "Mr. Johnson." "I cannot get on well without him."

"You will have to get on without him, if you take him to the North," the slave dealer persisted. "For I can tell you, stranger, as a friend: I'm an older man than you. I have seen lots of this world, and I reckon I've had more dealings with slaves than any man living or dead. I was once employed by General Wade Hampton for ten years doing nothing but breaking 'em in, and everybody knows that the General would not have a man that didn't understand his business. So I tell you, stranger, again, you had better sell and let me take that boy down to Orleans. He will do you no good if you take him across Mason's and Dixon's line. He is a keen boy, and I can see from the cut of his eye that he is certain to run away."

Ellen had to admit to herself that the obnoxious man was a good judge of character, but she simply said, "I think not, sir; I have great confidence in his fidelity."

"*Fidevil!*" the dealer cried indignantly as his fist came down on the edge of a saucer, upsetting a cup of hot coffee into another gentleman's lap.

The scalded man jumped up. "Don't disturb yourself, neighbor," said the slave dealer in a mild, polite tone; "accidents will happen in the best of families. It always makes me mad to hear a man talking about fidelity in slaves. There isn't a damned one of them who wouldn't take to his heels if he had half a chance."

Fortunately, "Mr. Johnson" did not have to answer him, for the steamer was then approaching Charleston, and everyone went out on deck.

The slave dealer, however, delighted with the attention he was getting, continued to speak to the crowd which gathered around him. "If I was the President of this mighty United States of America, the greatest and freest country in the whole universe, I would never let no man, I don't care who he is, take a slave into the North and bring him back here filled to the brim, as he is sure to be, with damned abolition vices, to taint all quiet slaves with the hellish spirit of running away.

"These are, Captain, my flat-footed, everyday, right up-and-down sentiments, and as this is a free country, Captain, I don't care who hears them, for I am a Southern man, every inch of me to the backbone!" At these words the crowd burst into three cheers for the South and for John C. Calhoun.

The speech and the cheers were more than "Mr. Johnson" could stand. "I fear the cold air on deck is too much for me," he explained to the captain, and went back into the cabin.

Upon entering the cabin, "Mr. Johnson" found at the breakfast table a young Southern military officer who had been on the same train. He also was traveling with a manservant. After greetings and some comments on the weather, the conversation turned to the usual subject of slaves.

"You will excuse me, sir," said the young officer, "for saying that I think you are very likely to spoil your boy by saying 'Thank you' to him. I assure you, sir, nothing spoils a slave so soon as saying 'Thank you' and 'If you please' to him. The only way to make a slave toe the mark and to keep him in his place is to storm at him like thunder and keep him trembling like a leaf. Don't you see that when I speak to my Ned he darts like lightning? If he didn't, I'd skin him."

Just then poor Ned came in, and the young officer swore at him fearfully to teach "Mr. Johnson" the proper way to treat his servant.

As Ned went out to fetch his master's luggage, the officer said, "The only way is to make slaves as humble as dogs; then they would never dare to run away."

The officer then advised "Mr. Johnson" not to go to

the North for his health, but to go instead to the warm springs at Arkansas, where his boy would be sure to stay in line.

"Thank you, sir, for your advice," answered "Mr. Johnson," "but I am quite sure that the air in Philadelphia will be best for me in my condition." Fortunately the officer did not know the condition "Mr. Johnson" suffered from was the one known as *slavery*, for which the only cure was Northern air.

At this point the ship pulled into the dock at Charleston. From the cabin Ellen and William looked at the crowd of people on the wharf. Was there someone among them who had been sent to find the escaping slaves? Or if not by design, would there be someone who would recognize William by chance?

Ellen and William remained on board until most of the passengers had debarked and the crowd was gone. Then William assisted his master ashore and hired a carriage to take them to the best hotel—the very hotel where John C. Calhoun and other Southern leaders stayed when they were in Charleston.

The hotel owner was most solicitous of "Mr. Johnson"; he had a slave escort him to a fine room, had the cook prepare poultices (a combination of bread, meal, and herbs, heated and placed in a cloth, to be applied as bandages), and had three slaves attend him at table when he went down to eat. William was given his dinner on a broken plate with a rusty knife and fork, and told to eat in the kitchen.

After dinner, "Mr. Johnson" paid the bill and generously tipped the servants who had helped him. "Your master is the finest gentleman who ever came to this hotel," one of them said to William, who silently agreed with all but two of the words he had spoken.

William and Ellen had planned to take a steamer from Charleston to Philadelphia. They found, however, that the steamer did not run during the winter months. They also heard that on its last voyage, a runaway slave had been found hiding on board and had been sent back to his master. Therefore William and Ellen were not sorry that they were to go by the Overland Mail Route, which involved taking a steamer for Wilmington, North Carolina, and a train from that point to Philadelphia. The change in plans, however, turned out to be the cause of some anxiety.

Upon leaving the hotel, William and Ellen had to go to the Charleston Custom House to get tickets for the steamer. There was a crowd of passengers in the Custom House. "Mr. Johnson" asked for tickets to Philadelphia for himself and his slave.

The chief customs officer, a mean-looking man, glared at them suspiciously. In a fierce tone of voice he said to William, "Boy, do you belong to that gentleman?"

William quickly replied, "Yes, sir."

As he handed the tickets to "Mr. Johnson," the man said, "I wish you to register your name here, sir, and the name of your boy, and pay a dollar duty on him."

Paying the dollar, "Mr. Johnson" pointed to his bandaged right arm and asked the officer to sign his name for him. This seemed to annoy the officer. Thrusting his hands deep into his pockets, he shouted with a bullying air, "I won't do it!"

This was a tense moment for the fugitives. The officer's loud tone attracted the attention of other passengers. Among them was the young military officer who had been so generous with his advice on the steamer to Charleston. He came over to "Mr. Johnson" as if they were old friends and said to the customs officer, "Mr. Johnson is my friend. I know him and his family like a book."

The captain of the steamer, who knew the young military officer, then came forward. "I will register the gentleman's name," he said in an offhand, sailorly manner; "I will take the responsibility upon myself."

When this had been done, the young military officer asked, "Won't you join me in a drink and a cigar?"

"Thank you, no. My health will not permit it," answered "Mr. Johnson," and, with his slave, boarded the ship.

"There was no disrespect to you intended," the captain later explained to "Mr. Johnson." "They are very careful at Charleston. I have known families with their slaves to be detained there for days until reliable information can be had about them. Otherwise these damned abolitionists could be stealing valuable slaves from the South any time they wanted to."

"I suppose so," agreed "Mr. Johnson," and thanked the captain for his help, trembling at the thought of how narrowly they had escaped being detained at Charleston —and sent back.

The next morning they reached Wilmington, North Carolina, where they boarded the train for Richmond, Virginia.

In the railroad car there was a compartment with two couches instead of seats, reserved for families or invalids, or for ladies traveling alone. The conductor, noticing that "Mr. Johnson" appeared to be ill, suggested that he ride in that compartment. An elderly gentleman and his two beautiful daughters were also ushered into that compartment. Before the train left the station, the old gentleman stepped into the car where the slaves rode to question William about his master. He wanted to know what was the matter with him, where he was from, and where he was going. William answered his questions. He then gave William a tip—ten cents—and urged him to take very good care of his master. This William readily promised to do—and he kept the promise for the rest of his life.

During the father's absence the young ladies had a pleasant conversation with "Mr. Johnson." When the father returned, he suggested that "Mr. Johnson" might feel better if he stretched out on the couch and rested. The ladies made an extra pillow of their shawls for his head. In order to avoid conversation, "Mr. Johnson" made believe he was asleep.

"Papa, he seems to be a very nice young gentleman," one of the young ladies commented.

"Oh, dear me," said her sister, "I never felt so drawn to a young gentleman in my life."

After a while, "Mr. Johnson" sat up and returned the shawls to the young ladies. When they were all seated, the ladies shared their refreshments with the stranger.

Just before the train reached Richmond, which was the family's destination, the old gentleman wrote out for "Mr. Johnson" a cure for rheumatism. "Mr. Johnson" thanked him, and put it immediately into his pocket, for fear that he might hold it upside down while pretending to read it.

Upon parting, the old gentleman gave him his card, containing his name and address, saying, "Please visit us if you come this way again. I shall be pleased to see you, and so will my daughters." "Mr. Johnson" promised to do so.

Ellen was both amused and relieved; evidently her

disguise was perfect. But her sense of security was to be short-lived. Very soon Ellen and William met a new crisis.

At Richmond a stout, elderly, aristocratic-looking lady entered the compartment. A young gentleman also came in. Suddenly the lady caught sight of William, who was standing on the platform, and jumped up. "Bless my soul," she exclaimed. "There goes my slave Tom."

"No," said "Mr. Johnson"; "that is my boy William."

The lady paid no attention to this but poked her head out of the window and shouted, "You, Tom, come here, you runaway rascal!"

William and Ellen had the same thought. Suppose the lady insisted that William was her Tom, and Ellen was asked to show her ownership papers!

Fortunately, as William came closer, the old lady looked at him again and said to "Mr. Johnson," "I beg your pardon, sir. I was sure he was Tom. I never in my life saw two black pigs more alike! I hope, sir, that your boy does not turn out to be so worthless as my Tom has. I could not have been kinder to him if he were my own son—and after all I did for him, he ran off for no reason about eighteen months ago."

"Did he have a wife?" asked the other gentleman.

"No, sir, not when he left, though he did have one a little before that. July was a beautiful girl, whiter than I am, but she became so ill after their baby died, that she was unable to do much work and I thought for her own good it would be better to sell her South. The New Orleans climate would be so much better for her. I asked my agent to be sure to sell her to a good master."

"I suppose she was very glad to go South for the restoration of her health," said the gentleman.

The lady, not recognizing the irony of the statement,

replied, "No, she was not, for they never know what's best for them. She and Tom carried on terribly, and soon after she was sold, he ran away for no reason. Within a few months, nine other slaves followed his example and ran away!"

"Why didn't you emancipate July, since she was too sick to work for you?" asked the young man. "My own mother emancipated all her slaves."

"I think that is a very unkind thing to do," replied the lady. "My husband directed in his will that all our slaves be emancipated, but my son and I thought he couldn't have been in his right mind, and we set aside the will. Setting them free would have been too unkind."

"Mr. Johnson" entered the conversation for the first time. "Do you mean, madam, unkind to them or unkind to you?" he asked.

"Unkind to them, of course, to expect them to shift for themselves when they are used to having us take such good care of them."

"My mother's slaves went to Ohio," asserted the young man, "where they are getting on very well. I saw some of them when I was there last summer."

The old lady's only reply was a sniff.

Shortly after this, the old lady reached her destination and left the train.

"What a shame it was," said the other young man, "for that mean, hypocritical old humbug to cheat the slaves out of their freedom! I hope they all run away!"

"Mr. Johnson" thought it best to make no comment.

The young man got off the train at the next station. Soon after that, Ellen and William left the train at Fredericksburg, where they boarded the steamer for Washington.

IV

The Last Giant Step

As THE SHIP approached Washington, the passengers did not become more tolerant. One ignorant, vulgar, tobacco-chewing man became enraged at the sight of the fine white felt hat which William had bought in order to make it harder to recognize him.

Turning to "Mr. Johnson," he said, "I reckon, stranger, you are spoiling that boy of yours, allowing him to wear such a devilish fine hat. Just look at the quality of it! The President couldn't wear a better one. I should just like to go and kick it overboard."

A friend touched him and said, "Don't speak so to a gentleman."

"Why not?" exclaimed the fellow fiercely. "It makes me itch all over to see slaves dressed like white men. Washington is run over with spoiled free blacks; if I had my way, I would sell every damned rascal of them way down South, where the devil would be whipped out of them."

"Mr. Johnson," upset by these words, walked off without answering.

In a few minutes, the ship landed at Washington, and there William and Ellen took a carriage to the train for Baltimore, the last slave port they were to see. They had left their cottage on Wednesday morning, the 21st of December. It was Christmas Eve, December 24, 1848, when they arrived in Baltimore.

William and Ellen were more tense than ever. They were so near their goal . . . yet they knew that officials in Baltimore were particularly watchful to prevent slaves from escaping across the border to Pennsylvania and freedom.

William settled his "master" in a first-class carriage on the train and went to the car in which blacks traveled. Before he entered, a Yankee officer stopped him, saying sternly, "Where are you going, boy?"

"Philadelphia, sir," William replied humbly.

"What are you going there for?" asked the officer.

"I am traveling with my master who is in another carriage, sir."

"I think you had better get him out, and be quick about it, because the train will soon be starting," the officer ordered. "It is against the rules to let any man take a slave past here unless he can satisfy them in the office that he has a right to take him along." The officer moved on, leaving William on the platform.

William's heart was beating furiously. To have come so far—and now this! How would Ellen be able to prove ownership? He consoled himself with the thought that God, who had been so good as to allow them to come this far, would not let them be turned aside now.

William hastened into the car to tell his master the bad news. "Mr. Johnson," seated comfortably in the railroad car, smiled at him. They were so near their destination.

"How are you feeling, sir?" asked William.

"Much better," answered his "master." "Thank God we are getting on so nicely."

"Not so nicely, sir, I am sorry to say," William said. "You must leave the train and convince the officials that I am your slave."

"Mr. Johnson" shuddered.

"Good heavens!" he whispered. "Is it possible that we will be sent back into slavery?"

They were silent for a few despairing moments. Then they left the train and made their way to the office.

Ellen summoned her last bit of courage.

"Do you wish to see me, sir?" "Mr. Johnson" asked the man who appeared to be the chief officer.

"Yes," he answered. "It is against our rules, sir, to allow any person to take a slave out of Baltimore into Philadelphia unless he can satisfy us that he has a right to take him along."

"Why is that?" asked "Mr. Johnson" innocently.

"Because, sir," the officer answered in a voice and manner that almost chilled the blood of the fugitives, "if we should allow any gentleman to take a slave past here into Philadelphia, and should the gentleman with whom the slave was traveling turn out to be not his rightful owner, and if the real owner should prove that his slave escaped on our railroad, we should have to pay for him."

This conversation attracted the attention of a large number of curious passengers. They seemed sympathetic to "Mr. Johnson," because he was so obviously ill.

Seeing the sympathy of the other passengers, the officer asked, more politely, "Do you know someone in

Baltimore who might vouch for you and assure us that you have a right to take this slave into Pennsylvania?"

"No, I do not," asserted "Mr. Johnson" regretfully. He then added more forcefully, "I bought tickets in Charleston to pass us through to Philadelphia, and you have no right to detain us here!"

The officer was firm. "Right or wrong, I shan't let you go."

William and Ellen looked at each other, but did not dare to say a word for fear they would give themselves away. They knew that, if the officer suspected them, he had the right to put them in prison. When their true identity became known, they would surely be sent back into slavery, and they knew they would rather be dead. They silently prayed to be delivered from this new danger.

Just then, the conductor of the train on which they had come from Washington, came in.

"Did this gentleman and his slave come on your train?" asked the official.

"They did," answered the conductor, and left.

Suddenly the bell rang for the train to leave. The other passengers fixed their eyes upon the officer, "Mr. Johnson," and his slave, their expressions showing their interest and concern.

The officer seemed agitated. Running his fingers through his hair, he finally said, "I don't know what to do." Then looking around, he added, "I calculate it is all right. Run and tell the conductor that it will be all right to let this gentleman and his slave proceed," he told one of the clerks. "Since he is not well, it is a pity to stop him here. We will let him go."

"Mr. Johnson" thanked him and stepped out, crossing the platform as quickly as possible, with his slave close

behind. William escorted his master into one of the best
carriages of the train and reached his own just as the
train pulled out.

It was eight o'clock on Christmas Eve, just eight days
after William had first thought of their plan. In the
four days before they left Macon, he and Ellen had both
been working; they had seen each other only at night,
when they talked over each detail of their plan. They
had had hardly any sleep for the four days of planning
and the four days of the journey. Now that the last
hurdle was passed, William realized how terribly tired
he was. Knowing that they would be in Philadelphia in
the morning, and that there were no important stations
between Baltimore and Philadelphia, William relaxed
his guard, and fell asleep. It proved to be the wrong
time for sleeping.

When the train reached Havre-de-Grace, all the first-
class passengers were told to get off the train and onto
a ferryboat, to be ferried across the Susquehanna River
to take the train again on the opposite side. This was to
spare the passengers the jolting of rolling the cars onto
the boat. The baggage cars, however, were rolled on the
boat to be taken off on the other side. The sleeping
William was near the baggage car, so they did not wake
him.

When Ellen left the railroad carriage to get on the
ferryboat, it was cold and dark and rainy. She was alone,
without William, for the first time on the journey. She
was frightened and confused.

"Have you seen my boy?" "Mr. Johnson" asked the
conductor.

The conductor, who may well have been an abolitionist, thought he would tease this Southern slaveowner.

"No, I haven't seen anything of him for some time;

no doubt he has run away and has reached Philadelphia long before now. He is probably a free man by now, sir."

"Mr. Johnson" knew better. "Please try to find him," he asked the conductor.

"I am no slave hunter," the conductor indignantly replied. "As far as I am concerned, everybody must look after his own slaves." With that, he strode away.

Ellen was frightened. She feared that Willam had been kidnaped into slavery, or perhaps killed on the train. She was in a predicament for another reason. She had no money at all. Although Ellen had been carrying the money up to then, she had given it all to William the night before after hearing that there were pick-pockets in Philadelphia who preyed on travelers. A pickpocket would not think of a slave as a likely victim.

Ellen did have the tickets, however. Frightened and confused though she was, she realized that there was no use in her staying there at Havre-de-Grace. She must board the ferry and complete her journey, hoping and praying that she and William would find each other again in freedom.

The ferry ride over, the passengers went back on the train. After the train was well on its way to Phila-delphia, the guard came to the car where William was sleeping and gave him a violent shake, saying, "Boy, wake up!"

William started, not knowing for a moment where he was.

"Your master is scared half to death about you," the guard continued. It was William's turn to be scared. He was sure that Ellen had been found out.

"What is the matter?" William managed to ask.

"Your master thinks you have run away from him," the guard explained.

Knowing that Ellen would never think any such thing, William felt reassured and went to his "master" immediately.

After talking with "Mr. Johnson" for a few minutes, William returned to his place, where the guard was talking with the conductor.

"What did your master want, boy?" asked the guard.

"He just wanted to know what had become of me."

"No," said the guard. "That's not it. He thought you had taken leave for parts unknown. I never saw a man so badly scared about losing his slave in my life. Now," continued the guard, "let me give you a little friendly advice. When you get to Philadelphia, run away and leave that cripple, and have your liberty."

"No, sir," replied William. "I can't promise to do that."

"Why not?" asked the conductor, evidently much surprised. "Don't you want your liberty?"

"Yes, sir," he replied, "but I shall never run away from such a good master as I have at present."

One of the men said to the guard, "Let him alone. I guess he'll open his eyes when he gets to Philadelphia."

In spite of William's seeming lack of interest, the men gave him a good deal of information about how to run away from his master in Philadelphia, information which he appeared not to be taking to heart, but which he found useful for both of them later.

On the train, William also met a free Negro, who recommended to him a boardinghouse in Philadelphia kept by an abolitionist, where he would be quite safe if he decided to run away from his master. William thanked him, but did not let him know who he and his "master" really were.

Later on in the night, William heard a fearful whistling of the steam engine; he looked out the window and saw many flickering lights. A passenger in the next car also stuck his head out the window and called to his companion, "Wake up! We are at Philadelphia." The sight of the city in the distance and the words he heard made William feel as if a burden had rolled off his back; he felt really happy for the first time in his life.

As soon as the train reached the platform, he went to get "Mr. Johnson," took their luggage, put it into a carriage, got in and drove off to the abolitionist's boardinghouse recommended to him by the free Negro.

No sooner had they left the station than Ellen, who had concealed her fears and played her part with so much courage and wit throughout the journey, grasped William's hand and said, "Thank God we are safe!" She burst into tears, and wept like a child.

When they reached the boardinghouse, Ellen was so weak and faint that she could scarcely stand alone. As soon as they were shown to their room, William and Ellen knelt down and thanked God for His goodness in enabling them to overcome so many dangers in escaping from slavery to freedom.

That was Sunday, December 25, Christmas Day of 1848.

Ellen was twenty-two years old, and William a few years older. They thought all their troubles were over. They were young, strong, and in love. And they were free.

But they had covered only the first thousand miles of their journey to freedom. Something was to happen two years later that extended that journey by three thousand miles more.

Trembling, Ellen took off the cloak, high-heeled boots, and black suit which she had worn for four days and, with a sigh of relief, put on her own clothing. She and

William then went downstairs to meet the owner of the boardinghouse.

Free and happy at last, they luckily did not know what the future held in store for them.

V

The Land of the (Almost) Free: Philadelphia

ELLEN AND WILLIAM went downstairs and asked to see the proprietor of the boardinghouse. When that gentleman entered, he was astonished to find a strange young woman.

"Where is your master?" he asked William.

"There," said William, pointing to Ellen.

"I am not joking," the proprietor said. "I really wish to see your master."

William again pointed to Ellen. At first the man could not believe his eyes.

"That is surely not the gentleman who came with you," he insisted.

William then confessed that they were fugitive slaves and told him how they had escaped.

"I have welcomed many fugitive slaves to Philadelphia," said the boardinghouse owner, "but I've never heard of an escape like yours. You know," he added,

"Philadelphia is, for many fugitives, the first stop on the Underground Railroad."

Ellen and William looked puzzled. They had come by railroad and boat. But—"*Underground* railroad?" they repeated.

"That's what we call the escape route for slaves: they are guided from one friendly house to another, and hidden until it is safe to go farther North. The law requires that fugitive slaves be sent back to their masters, just as any stolen property should be restored. You're not entirely safe, even here. That is why many slaves go along the underground railroad until they reach Canada where they are free."

"What do you think we should do now? Is it safe for us to stay in Philadelphia for a while?"

"I don't know. I am not an expert in these matters, but I will invite some abolitionist leaders to meet you. They will be able to advise you. Rest a while. I'll be back soon."

A short time later, their host returned with several men—the first abolitionists William and Ellen had ever seen. Among them was Mr. William Still, a free Negro who was introduced to them as the Chairman of the Acting Vigilant Committee of the Philadelphia Branch of the Underground Railroad. Another of their visitors was Mr. Robert Purvis, President of the Underground Railroad Society and Vice-President of the Anti-Slavery Society.

William and Ellen learned later of Robert Purvis's connection with slavery. Although his father was English, and his mother a free-born American, his mother's mother had been kidnaped in Morocco and sold into slavery with a shipload of Africans when she was twelve years old. His grandmother's mistress was very fond of her little slave and emancipated her; she later married a Jewish man named Baron Judah. Mr. Purvis's mother was their daughter. Although all of Robert Purvis's ancestors except this one grandmother had been free, he devoted his life, after graduating from Amherst College, to the anti-slavery cause. His home was one of the stations on the Underground Railroad. In it there was a secret room, a room without any doors or windows. It could be entered only from a trapdoor in the ceiling of the room below. There Mr. Purvis harbored fugitive slaves who were in danger of being caught.

Mr. Purvis and the other men who came to see the Crafts were astounded by their story. They asked to see Ellen in her disguise. She obligingly went to her room and soon reappeared as the young white Southern gentleman who had entered the boardinghouse just a few hours earlier. Ellen, who hated her disguise, hurried to change back into her own clothing.

While she was upstairs, William asked the visitors for advice. "Shall we stay here?" William asked.

"No, Philadelphia is too near the slave states; it is a good first stop, but it would not be a good place to settle," answered Mr. Still.

"Ellen and I had thought of going to Canada. What do you think?" William asked.

"Many fugitives do go on to Canada," replied Mr. Purvis. "You would be completely safe there."

Mr. Still interposed, "I don't think it is a good place for the Crafts now. It is December, and they have just come from a warm climate. Canada would be too cold." Turning to William, he added, "I should suggest your going to Boston."

William was hesitant. "Could we not be caught and sent back into slavery from Boston?"

"According to the law, yes. But there are so many prominent abolitionists in Boston—Wendell Phillips, Charles Sumner, Theodore Parker, Lewis Hayden—and their influence is so strong that no slave hunter has been able to get a slave out of Boston."

"Why don't you stay in Philadelphia for a few weeks until Mrs. Craft recovers from her ordeal, and you get used to the cold weather?" suggested Mr. Still.

A dark-complexioned, quiet gentleman who had not spoken before, turned to William. "Thee and thy wife could stay with me and my family on our farm for a while." The man who spoke was introduced as Mr. Barkley Ivens. His addressing William as *thee* instead of *you* indicated that Mr. Ivens was a member of the Society of Friends, known as Quakers.

At this point Ellen returned to the room—a beautiful young lady again.

"Ellen, Mr. Ivens has invited us to stay with him and his family on his farm for a while. Would you like to do that?"

Ellen nodded yes.

"We shall be most grateful to accept your invitation," William said, and received instructions about how to get to the farm.

The visitors soon departed, leaving William and Ellen to marvel at the distinguished positions members of their race had attained in Philadelphia, and at the warm welcome they, who had been slaves only the day before, had received.

After a few days, the fugitives set forth for the Ivens farm. They took a steamer up the Delaware River to a landing, where they were met by Mr. Ivens, who helped them into his snug little cart and drove them to his home. William thought he would never forget Mr. Ivens' invitation—the first great service ever done him by a white person.

It turned out, however, that Ellen did not share this view.

She had thought the dark-complexioned Mr. Ivens was, like Mr. Still and Mr. Purvis, of African or slave ancestry. As the cart came near the house, she saw Mrs. Ivens, small, plump, and smiling, standing at the door with her daughters. They were white.

"I'll take the luggage; you go into the house and make yourselves comfortable," Mr. Ivens said.

But Ellen was afraid to move. Standing in the yard, she whispered to William, "I thought we were going among our own people."

"It is all right, Ellen," William assured her. "These are the same."

"No, they are not," Ellen insisted. "I am not going to stay here. I have no confidence whatever in white people; they will surely send us back into slavery."

Ellen turned and started for the road.

Mrs. Ivens quickly came down to her, and took her hand. "How art thou, my dear? We are all very glad to see thee and thy husband. Come in to the fire. I daresay thou art cold and hungry after thy journey."

Ellen consented to be led to the house, but said, "I shall only stay a little while."

"But where art thou going this cold night?" asked Mr. Ivens, who had just entered the room.

"I don't know," answered Ellen in a dejected voice.

"Well then, I think thou hadst better take off thy things and sit near the fire. Tea will soon be ready," Mr. Ivens said, trying to reassure Ellen.

"Come, Ellen," added Mrs. Ivens. "Let me assist thee." She began to untie Ellen's bonnet strings. "Don't be frightened, my dear," she said. "I shall not hurt a hair of thy head. We have heard with much pleasure of the marvelous escape of thee and thy husband. I don't wonder at thee being timid, poor thing, but thou needst not fear us. We would as soon send one of our daughters into slavery as thee."

Ellen, touched by Mrs. Ivens' kindness, began to cry. She felt her fears and prejudices begin to melt away.

Soon Sally Ann, the Ivens' housekeeper, and Jacob, their houseman, both free Negroes, brought in the tea things. William talked to them, and they assured him that he and his wife would be safe and happy in the Ivens' home.

After they finished tea, Mrs. Ivens asked William and Ellen whether they knew how to read and write. When they said they did not she and her daughters offered to teach them.

Slates, pencils, and copybooks quickly took the place of teacups and saucers. But William and Ellen looked at each other mournfully. They knew how hard it had been for them to learn the letters of the alphabet by themselves.

"We are afraid we are too old to begin," William said apologetically. "We will be wasting your time."

"Not at all," Mrs. Ivens assured him. "It is never too late to learn." They began the lessons that very minute. By the time Ellen and William's visit with the Ivens ended, they knew the written alphabet, as well as the printed, and could write their names.

Although Ellen and William were comfortable and happy with the Ivens, they wanted to find a permanent home and begin to earn a living. They decided to go on to Boston. When they left the peaceful farm, Ellen, who only three weeks before had been afraid to enter the house, felt that she was parting from her own family. She and William knew that they would never forget the Ivens, and their gentle, warm kindness to fugitives.

Since William had not yet spent all the money he had earned and saved in slavery, he was able to buy tickets to Boston. This time Ellen and William rode together in the train. The trip was not dangerous, but their future was still uncertain. The wheels, clattering along the rails, seemed to be saying, "What next? What next? What next?"

VI

Boston: City of Refuge?

BOSTON was a proud city, with a history of freedom. It was called *The Hub*, as if it were the center of a wheel, with spokes radiating outward to the rest of the country. The spokes could be thought of as ideas, trade, books, politics, religious philosophies. Or the spokes could be named for the Boston heroes—among them Paul Revere, who had warned that the British were coming; Crispus Attucks, a black man, who was the first person to give his life in the Boston Massacre which marked the beginning of the American Revolution; and John Adams, who helped to write the Declaration of Independence and later became President of the United States.

In 1849 when the Crafts came to Boston, there were new heroes in the city, who were once again exhibiting the independence of their ancestors. These were the abolitionists, who fought with words and deeds against slavery, and who protected all fugitive slaves who came to their great city. Among their leaders were William

Lloyd Garrison, editor of *The Liberator;* Wendell Phillips, a brilliant lawyer; Phillips' friend Lewis Hayden, a distinguished black lawyer; Frederick Douglass, an ex-slave and abolitionist leader; Thomas Wentworth Higginson, a white man who later became Colonel of the first black regiment in the Civil War; and the Reverend Theodore Parker, a minister who was to become the chief friend and protector of Ellen and William Craft.

With such men as these to protect fugitive slaves, William and Ellen felt safe in Boston. They found lodgings and began to work—William as a cabinet-maker, his wages now going to no one but himself, and Ellen as a seamstress, sewing for their friends.

Although Boston was a city of refuge for escaped slaves, the condition of its black citizens was far from ideal. Most of them lived in an old and crowded section of the western part of Boston; no matter where they lived, they had to send their children to the segregated Smith School—known to be of inferior quality.

In 1844 a group of Boston Negroes complained about the Smith School and its principal, and were disappointed when the school board, with only two dissenters, acquitted the principal of the charges against him. They then drew up a resolution against segregated schools.

A year later a committee appointed by the school board to examine all the schools reported that the Smith School was in "deplorable condition." The children were learning very little; although they were able to recite some facts from memory without understanding them, topics which might have been of interest, such as the geography and politics of the West Indies and the African nations from which the children's ancestors had come, were not taught. Only one or two children knew about the Emancipation Act, by which England had freed the slaves in its territories. The committee believed, however, that "there is enough good sense among the parents, and enough intellect among the children" to make the school a good one if it had proper leadership.

Nevertheless, segregation and inferior education continued. In 1849, the year of the Crafts' arrival in Boston, Benjamin Roberts, a Negro, tried to enroll his five-year-old daughter Sarah in a white primary school in the district in which he lived. She was rejected, on the basis of her color. Mr. Roberts then sued the city of Boston. His lawyer was Charles Sumner, a leading abolitionist who later became a United States Senator. Mr. Roberts lost his case, but six years later, Boston abolished separate schools for Negroes.

To offset instances of discrimination against Negroes were instances of real friendship. When Frederick Douglass, ex-slave, and his white friend Wendell Phillips traveled together, Phillips rode with Douglass in the filthy "Jim Crow" car, saying, "If you cannot ride with me, I can ride with you." According to Douglass, "On the Sound, between New York and Newport, in those dark days, a colored passenger was not allowed abaft the wheels of the steamer, and had to spend the night on the forward deck, with horses, sheep, and swine. On such trips, when I was a passenger, Wendell Phillips preferred to walk the naked deck with me to taking a stateroom. I could not persuade him to leave me to bear the burden of insult and outrage alone."

When Harvard College admitted its first Negro student, the white students threatened to leave. The President of the College stated that they could leave if they wished, but that if all of them withdrew, all the resources of the College would be devoted to the education of one Negro student.

In this city of light and shadow, of friendship and bigotry, William and Ellen settled happily. In time their story might have been forgotten.

William and Ellen were not content, however, to live in safety while their families and friends and many others of their race remained in slavery. Therefore, they joined their abolitionist friends at anti-slavery meetings, to tell, as Frederick Douglass was doing, the first-hand story of what it meant to be a slave. There was danger for the Crafts in becoming conspicuous, but they had never shrunk from danger.

Years later, when someone praised the abolitionists as having been persuasive public speakers, Thomas Wentworth Higginson wrote: "I know that my own teachers were the slave women who came shyly before the audience. . . . What were the tricks of oratory in the face of men and women like these? We learned to speak because their presence made silence impossible."

The Crafts had been in Boston less than a month when they spoke at an anti-slavery meeting that was reported in the newspapers. An article appeared in the Connecticut *New Haven Register* about the meeting. At that time newspaper editors often got their news from other papers. The article about the Crafts was reprinted in the *Macon* (Georgia) *Telegraph*, which added the following comment: "The Mr. and Mrs. Craft who figure so largely in the above paragraphs will be recognized at once by our city readers as the slaves belonging to Dr. Collins and Mr. Ira H. Taylor of this place, who ran away or were decoyed from their owners in December last."

William's and Ellen's owners now knew where their

slaves could be found, but they took no immediate action. They knew it was almost impossible to get a fugitive slave out of Boston. They bided their time.

The Crafts, in the meantime, lived and worked happily in Boston; they felt no sense of impending doom. After getting used to their surroundings, and finding employment and a place to live, they were ready to go on with their studies. They learned of a night school which they could attend. The first session was to be held on a certain night in October, 1850. But circumstances occurred which not only prevented them from going to school that night, but even led to their being forced to leave the city of Boston.

On September 18, 1850, the President of the United States, Millard Fillmore, had signed into law the Fugitive Slave Bill, which had just been passed by Congress. According to this law anyone who helped a fugitive slave in any way was liable to a fine of one thousand dollars and a term of six months in jail. If the slave succeeded in escaping, whoever helped him also had to pay one thousand dollars to the owner to compensate for his lost property. If a man accused of being a fugitive slave was brought into court, he was not allowed to testify in his own defense. The judge who decided whether the accused was slave or free received a fee—ten dollars, if he decided the accused was a slave—five dollars if he decided the accused was free. Once the prisoner was judged to be a slave, he was turned over to a United States marshal, whose duty it was to restore him to his owners, with the help of the United States Army if necessary.

All of this made it much easier for slave hunters or slave-owners to kidnap free blacks into slavery or to recover escaped slaves.

There was consternation among the Negroes in Boston and in other cities in which they had made their homes. Within three days of the signing of the law, forty Negroes left their Boston homes, their work, and their friends to flee northward to Canada. Theodore Parker and the anti-slavery group promised them protection if they stayed—but how could they be sure of success?

A Vigilance Committee, such as had been formed earlier to protect fugitive slaves, was formed again, with Theodore Parker at the head. One hundred and sixty-three people joined immediately; within a few days there were two hundred and fifty members. At a meeting these members drew up resolutions opposing the Fugitive Slave Law, declaring that it was unconstitutional, because it did not do those things which the Constitution of the United States was formed to do: it did not "tend to form a more perfect union, establish justice, ensure domestic tranquillity, provide for the common defense, promote the general welfare, or secure the blessings of liberty to the people. . . ."

The Resolution went on to urge the fugitive slaves to remain in Boston and to encourage those who had fled to return; the members promised to establish vigilance committees to protect them.

Some of the lawyers formed a legal committee whose duty it was to be on the watch, and find out when a warrant was taken out for the arrest of a fugitive. (This they did by having a sympathetic spy in the marshal's office.) They then warned the fugitive, and took whatever measures were necessary to insure his safety. If the fugitive was caught and brought before a judge, they saw to it that he had a lawyer, and that all legal delaying tactics were made use of; if he was judged to be a slave, then the public was to be informed, so that they could help him escape. Helping a fugitive, they announced, was to be more important than any other work of any of the members of the Vigilance Committee.

Among the first fugitive slaves who needed help were Ellen and William Craft. Their owners, Dr. Collins and Mr. Taylor, did not wait long to take advantage of the new law. Just a month after the enactment of the law, in October, 1850, William Craft had an unexpected visitor in his shop—John Knight, a white man, a carpenter, who had worked with him in the shop in Macon. John, acting as if he had found William by chance, greeted him warmly. William responded warily.

"What are you doing in Boston?" William asked.

"Just visiting."

"Did you come alone?"

"Yes. How about coming out and showing me the town?"

"I'm very busy, as you can see. Perhaps some other time."

After asking about Ellen, John said he'd drop in again the next day. William told Ellen about his visitor. They decided that William would go to work as usual, but under no circumstances would he go out with John Knight. William also bought a revolver so as to defend himself if necessary.

The following day John came again and asked William in an offhand manner whether he would just go for a little walk with him on Boston Common. Again William said he had too much work to do, and could not spare the time.

"I can see that you're very busy. Perhaps the evening would be a better time. Why don't you bring Ellen to see me at my hotel—the United States Hotel. I can give Ellen news of her mother, and if you want to send a message, I'll take it."

William and Ellen did not avail themselves of that invitation. The following day William received a letter from Knight:

WILLIAM CRAFT.—SIR,—I have to leave so eirley in the morning that I cold not call according to promis, so if you want me to carry a letter home with me, you must bring it to the United states Hotel tomorro and leave it in box 44, or come yourself tomorro evening after tea and bring it. Let me no if you come by yourself by sending a note to box 44 U.S.hotel, so that I may no whether to wate after tea or not by the bearer. If your wif wants to see me you cold bring her with you if you come yourself,

JOHN KNIGHT

P.S. I shall leave for home eirley a Thursday morning.

—J.K.

William questioned the messenger who brought him this letter. "Was the gentleman who sent the letter alone?"

"No, another man was with him."

Needless to say, William did not fall for this trick.

In the meantime the members of the Vigilance Committee learned the identity of the slave-catcher from their spy in the marshal's office. He was Willis Hughes, a jailer from Macon, Georgia, who had been sent to Boston by Dr. Collins and Mr. Taylor with warrants for the arrest of Ellen and William Craft. He had brought John Knight with him to identify William, and, he hoped, to trick him, so as not to alert the Vigilance Committee.

As soon as he heard about Hughes, Dr. Samuel Gridley Howe, (the husband of Julia Ward Howe, author of "The Battle Hymn of the Republic") a physician who was best known for his work with the blind, left his work and hurried to the home of Theodore Parker to inform him of the danger to the Crafts.

Mr. Parker put aside the sermon he was writing. "We must hide William and Ellen until we can get rid of the slave catchers," Parker said, and together Howe and he planned two courses of action—to find hiding places for William and Ellen, and to prevent Hughes from serving the warrant.

They asked Mrs. Hilliard, wife of one of the Commissioners, to take Ellen into her home. Mrs. Hilliard went to the shop where Ellen was learning to do upholstery, and not wishing to alarm Ellen, simply asked her to come to her house to do some sewing for her.

"I'll be able to come some day next week," Ellen said.

"No, you must come immediately! I need you," Mrs. Hilliard insisted.

Ellen knew that this was not like the gentle Mrs. Hilliard.

"What is wrong?" Ellen asked. "I know something must be wrong."

Mrs. Hilliard had to tell her that slave catchers had come from Georgia and that she and William had been right to be suspicious of the seemingly friendly John Knight. Now that Knight's trickery had failed to work, Mrs. Hilliard and the members of the Vigilance Committee were sure that Hughes' next step would be to go to the Crafts' home to serve the warrant and arrest them.

"Mr. Parker thinks that you should come to my house

to hide," Mrs. Hilliard said. "He will find a hiding place for William too until we can get rid of the slave hunters."

Ellen, however, refused to go with Mrs. Hilliard. "Your husband is a commissioner who is supposed to uphold the law—even a law as horrible as the Fugitive Slave Law. There would be a scandal if he were found sheltering fugitive slaves in his house. I cannot put him in that position."

Mrs. Hilliard insisted, "But, Ellen, you know that my husband is against slavery. I have hidden fugitive slaves in our attic many times, with his full knowledge and consent."

Ellen stubbornly refused; another place had to be found. Theodore Parker, John Parkman and Miss Hannah Stevenson, an elderly friend who lived with the Parkers, serving as secretary and housekeeper, drove Ellen out of town to the home of Ellis Gray Loring—the nonviolent Mr. Parker carrying an axe in his hand! They were greeted at the door by a young lady who said, "I am Mary Carson, Mrs. Loring's niece. My aunt and uncle are away for a few days. May I take a message for them?"

"No, thank you. No message." Mr. Parker hesitated, then said, "I have Ellen Craft waiting in the carriage. I must leave her here in hiding. Mrs. Loring has offered her protection whenever it should be needed. May I leave her here with you?"

Mary Carson readily agreed. After impressing upon Miss Carson the need for secrecy, Mr. Parker and Miss Stevenson left.

Mary and Ellen liked each other at first sight. The following day, Ellen helped Mary make a new dress. Mary knew how worried Ellen must be about William, and she admired Ellen's self-control.

Mrs. Loring returned that afternoon, and she too made Ellen feel welcome.

Late in the afternoon a messenger came from Boston to tell Ellen that William was safe; he was well-armed, and staying at home. Somewhat reassured, Ellen spent a quiet evening and another busy day with Mary and Mrs. Loring.

The following evening, Sunday, Dr. Henry Bowditch, a member of the Vigilance Committee, came to the Loring home, bringing William with him.

"You must stay here with Ellen and get some rest," he told William, who was exhausted after sitting up armed for several nights, waiting for the Georgia jailer, Willis Hughes.

"You had better go up to Ellen's room, and don't either of you leave the room unless you know that no stranger is here," Dr. Bowditch cautioned William.

William and Ellen went upstairs together. A few minutes later Ellen called to Mrs. Loring, asking her please to come up to their room.

After greeting Mrs. Loring and thanking her for her kindness to Ellen, William said, "Ellen has just told me that Mr. Loring is not at home, and that he does not know that we are here. I cannot stay without his knowledge, because we are subjecting him to a heavy fine and imprisonment. We must leave at once."

Mrs. Loring assured William that her husband was part of the Vigilance Committee, and would want to help them in any way possible.

"Nevertheless, I cannot stay without his knowledge," William insisted. Mrs. Loring had to give them a guide to another house in the neighborhood, where the host and hostess were at home and would shelter them. The following morning it became known to others that the

Crafts were in that neighborhood; they were no longer safe there, and had to go back to Boston.

Ellen was taken to the home of Theodore Parker, where she stayed for a week. On the alert for the slave hunters, Mr. Parker kept a pistol beside him while he sat at his desk writing his sermons and keeping a diary in which he jotted down all the events of the day.

William, meanwhile, was being sheltered in the home of Lewis Hayden.

The second part of Parker's plan—to get rid of the slave hunters—had already been put into operation. The public was informed of the presence and the identity of Hughes and Knight by means of printed posters which contained the words SLAVE HUNTERS, the names of Knight and Hughes, and descriptions of both men. Members of the Vigilance Committee were assigned to follow them everywhere. Other sympathizers recognized them also, and jeers and cries of "Slave Hunters! Go back to Georgia!" followed them wherever they went.

The Legal Committee got out a warrant for the arrest of Hughes on charges not only of conspiracy to kidnap, but also of slander, because he had called William Craft a thief who had stolen himself and the clothes he wore from his owner. Hughes was arraigned in court, where the judge set his bail at ten thousand dollars—a very large sum. The bail was soon paid by a Boston merchant —a member of the Reverend Mr. Parker's congregation—and Hughes was free to leave. John Knight was also in the courtroom at this time, and when the session ended, he escaped by a rear door. But Hughes emerged from the court right into a crowd of abolitionists. As he hurried into a waiting carriage, a Negro brandishing a revolver jumped up, smashed the rear window, and was about to shoot Hughes when a nonviolent member of the Committee, probably Parker, pulled him away. To calm the black man, he said, "I will not let you have his murder on your conscience! I have heard that Hughes is planning to leave Boston tomorrow morning. We will see to it that he does."

At six o'clock the following morning, Parker, Francis Channing, Charles Ellis, and other members of the Vigilance Committee, about twenty in all, went to the United States Hotel to see Hughes. Despite the early hour, the landlord said that Hughes was not in. "We will wait for him," said Parker firmly.

Mr. Parker walked about for a while, then asked a clerk whether Hughes and Knight were in.

"If you will send up your name, we will see."

Mr. Parker sent a note; soon the clerk returned with a slip of paper on which was scrawled, "Mr. Hughes is *inguage*" (meaning engaged, or busy).

Fearing that Hughes and Knight would escape, Mr. Parker stationed himself at the door to Room 44 and asked two men to stand guard at the stairways. The landlord, however, insisted that Parker leave his post, and finally, he was taken up to see Hughes.

Parker assured Hughes that he had come as a minister to urge him, in friendship, to leave Boston at once.

"But we came here to execute the law," Hughes insisted.

"You must realize by now," said Parker, "that you cannot arrest William and Ellen Craft, and that if you do, you will never be able to take them out of the city of Boston."

Reluctantly, Hughes agreed to leave.

Both Hughes and Knight then complained to Parker

about the way they had been treated. Knight said he was not a slave hunter; he had simply come with Hughes. Yet he too had been jeered at and mobbed.

Parker turned to Hughes. "You are not safe in Boston another night," he warned. "I have stood between you and violence once. I cannot promise to do so again."

"We were planning to leave this morning at 7:30— but when we went down, there was a mob in front of the hotel—forty or fifty fellows hurrahing, and swinging their caps, and calling out, 'Slave hunters! There goes the slave hunters!' "

"We are here to give you safe conduct," Parker assured them. "But you must leave at once; I was able to prevent bloodshed only because you had arranged to leave this morning."

Hughes was surly. "We don't want your safe-conduct. We can take care of ourselves. We will leave sometime today," he added grudgingly.

And they did; not daring to board the train in Boston, Hughes and Knight stole out of the city and went to Newton Corner where they boarded the train for New York at two o'clock that afternoon.

Ellen and William Craft were still in danger, however. Anyone could capture them and claim a reward. Or their owners might send other messengers to catch them.

A wealthy Boston merchant offered to rescue them. "Give yourselves up, and I promise to buy you from your owners and set you free—no matter what the cost."

It was a tempting offer. If William and Ellen were free, they could remain in Boston among their friends; as things were now, they would have to flee from the United States, for they were not safe anywhere within its borders.

Yet, after thinking about it and talking it over with Ellen and others, William refused. "There are two or three hundred fugitive slaves in Boston. They cannot all be purchased from their masters and set free. Ellen and I will share their fate. If my freedom could be bought for two cents," William said, "I would not permit you to pay it."

It was decided that the Crafts should escape to England. A ship was due to leave Boston for Liverpool within a week—yet it would not be safe for the Crafts to try to board it. The warrant for their arrest was still in effect. The harbor was watched, and every ship searched for fugitive slaves. The Vigilance Committee took precautions even in the harbor. The sympathetic Captain Bearse had his yacht, the *Flirt*, anchored in Boston Harbor ready to rescue fugitive slaves who came hidden in ships from the South, and to help those escaping from Boston to board ships to Europe. It was too hazardous, however, for the Crafts to make the attempt. They and their friends decided that they should leave Boston secretly and make their way to Portland, Maine, where they could secretly board the ship for England.

VII

Bible, Bowie Knife, and Flight

BEFORE Ellen and William left for England, they asked
Theodore Parker to marry them. They had been married
in Georgia after the slave fashion, but had never had a
legal certificate or a religious ceremony. Mr. Parker told
William how to go about getting "a certificate of pub-
lication" as required by the new law of Massachusetts.

On November 7th, at 11 a.m., Theodore Parker married Ellen and William in a boarding house in Boston.

It was Mr. Parker's practice to talk to the bride and
groom before he performed the marriage ceremony. He
told William and Ellen what he usually told the young
couples whom he married about love and trust and the
obligations of marriage. Then he added, "William, your
position demands special duties of you. You are an out-
law; there is no law in the United States which protects
your liberty. You are protected only by the public opinion of men and women in Boston—and by your own
strength. If a man attacks you, intending to return you

to slavery, you have a right, a natural right, to resist the man unto death; yet you might refuse to exercise that right for *yourself*. You might let yourself be taken back into slavery rather than hurt or kill the slave hunter who attacks you. But your wife is dependent upon you. It is your duty to protect her, and this is a duty which you cannot refuse. I charge you, therefore, if the worst comes to the worst, to defend the life and the liberty of Ellen, your wife, against any slave hunter, even though in doing so you dig your own grave and the grave of a thousand men."

Mr. Parker then performed the marriage ceremony, closing with a prayer for their future happiness. The minister then picked up a Bible which was lying on one table, and a Bowie knife (a Western sword) lying on another. Placing the Bible in William's hand, he said, "This book contains the noblest truths in the possession of the human race. Read it and ponder it. With this book you will save your own soul and your wife's soul."

Mr. Parker put the knife into William's right hand, and said: "As you know, I am a man of peace and opposed to violence. Therefore do not use this sword unless there is no other way to protect your wife's liberty. Even as you use it, do not hate the man you strike, for if you do, your action will be sinful." The Reverend Parker blessed the couple, praying that their future would be as happy as their past had been difficult.

After this strange ceremony, the Crafts began their roundabout journey to England.

Theodore Parker was not content to have helped the Crafts escape. He wanted to change the law of the land. As a minister, he obeyed the law of the Old Testament: "Thou shalt not deliver unto his master the servant which is escaped from his master unto thee. He shall dwell with thee, even among you, in that place which he shall choose in one of thy gates, where it liketh him best; thou shalt not oppress him."

Two weeks after the wedding, Mr. Parker wrote a long letter to President Fillmore. He introduced himself as a minister who had a bad reputation among many in the city and throughout the country:

I have a large religious society in this town, composed of "all sorts and conditions of men," fugitive slaves who do not legally own the nails on their fingers and cannot read the Lord's Prayer, and also men and women of wealth and fine cultivation. I wish to inform you of the difficulty in which we (the church and myself) are placed by the new Fugitive Slave Law. There are several fugitive slaves in the society. They have committed no wrong; they have the same "unalienable right" to life, liberty, and the pursuit of happiness that you have; they naturally look to me for advice in their affliction. They are strangers, and ask me to take them in; hungry, and beg me to feed them; they are naked, and look to me for clothing; sick, and wish me to visit them. . . .

But *your* law will punish me with fine of 1,000 dollars and imprisonment for six months if I take in one of these strangers, feed and clothe these naked and hungry children of want; nay, if I visit them when they are sick, come unto them when they are in prison, or help them "directly or indirectly" when they are ready to perish . . .

I would rather lie all my life in a gaol [jail] and starve there, than refuse to protect one of these parishioners of mine. . . .

William Craft and Ellen were parishioners of mine; they have been at my house, I married them a fortnight ago this day; after the ceremony I put a Bible and a sword into William's hands, and told him the use of each. When the slave hunters were here, suppose I had helped the man to escape out of their hands; suppose I had taken the woman to my own house, and sheltered her there till the storm had passed by; should *you* think I had done a thing worthy of fine and imprisonment? If I took all *peaceful* measures to thwart the kidnapers (legal kidnapers) of their prey, would that be a thing for punishment? You cannot think that I am to stand by and see my own church carried off to slavery and do nothing to hinder such a wrong?

There hangs beside me in my library, as I write, the gun my grandfather fought with at the Battle of Lexington—he was a captain on that occasion—and also the musket he captured from a British soldier on that day—the first taken in the War for Independence. If I would not peril my property, my liberty, nay, my life, to keep my own parishioners out of slavery, then I would throw away those trophies, and should think I was the son of some coward, and not a brave man's child.

Mr. Parker enclosed one of his anti-slavery sermons. President Fillmore did not answer Theodore Parker's letter. It was many years before the answer came from another President—in the form of the Emancipation Proclamation.

There was another letter about the Crafts, however, to which President Fillmore did respond. Dr. Robert Collins, Ellen's former owner, wrote to the President protesting the treatment that his agent, Willis Hughes, had received in Boston, and the failure of the Boston officers to return his property to him. The President answered through the Acting Secretary of the State Department that he had ordered the sending of United States troops to assist the officers in arresting the Crafts.

By the time these letters were received by President Fillmore, however, Ellen and William Craft had left the inhospitable land of their birth.

VIII

England's Green and
Pleasant Land

THE SHIP which the Crafts did not dare to board in Boston was due to stop at Portland, Maine. In order to insure Ellen and William's safety, the Reverend Samuel May, Jr. accompanied them on the train to Portland. He thought they might need his help, because officers of the law often rode the trains to find fugitive slaves and return them to the owners. (This practice was so prevalent that the antislavery directors of the Syracuse and Utica Railroad had ordered their agents not to sell tickets to an officer who had a fugitive slave in custody, and not to allow such officers and slaves to ride on the train. The employees of the railroad were directed to try to help fugitive slaves to escape from their captors.)

The Crafts and Mr. May arrived in Portland without incident, only to find that the ship which they planned to board had collided with a schooner the night before, and was lying up for repairs.

William and Ellen had to stay in Portland. They were

welcomed at the home of Daniel Oliver, a generous and kind-hearted abolitionist, but they hated to stay there, for they knew they were subjecting their host to fine and imprisonment. Nevertheless the Olivers insisted that they stay, and made them feel at home.

The delay at this time, however, when Ellen and William should have been on a ship bound for England, soon became intolerable. They determined to go on to Canada and there board the ship to Liverpool.

Samuel May, before leaving them, gave them a letter to a fellow minister, Dr. Estlin of Bristol, England, in which he described the Crafts and their heroism, and asked Dr. Estlin to welcome them to England and do all he could for them.

At Portland, the Crafts took a steamer for St. Johns, New Brunswick.

When they set foot on Canadian soil, they breathed sighs of relief. They had escaped from the Fugitive Slave Law and its enforcers. They were disappointed to find, however, that Canada suffered from the same disease as its neighbor, the United States. In this new country also they met prejudice directed at them because of their skin color.

The Crafts had to wait two days for the steamer that was to take them from St. Johns to Windsor, Nova Scotia. At the first hotel they entered in St. Johns, the manager told them he had plenty of room for the lady (thinking her white) but as to William—"We never take in colored folks."

"Don't worry about me," William said. "If you have room for the lady, that will do. Just take the luggage up to the room." William went for a little walk, then returned and asked to see the lady. Ellen ordered dinner for two. The porter could not imagine that her eating companion was to be William.

"Would you like it now, or will you wait for your friend?" he asked.

To the surprise of the servants, Ellen and William ate together.

The landlord, who was away at the time of this incident, had learned from the steward of the ship the Crafts had come on that the Crafts were going on to England. Since the landlord was English, he was pleased to hear this, and, unlike the servants, treated the Crafts with great courtesy.

Two days later the steamer arrived, and the Crafts left for Windsor. There they found a coach bound for Halifax, Nova Scotia, where the ship from Boston would stop on its way to England. Prejudice against color forced William to sit on top of the coach in the rain, while Ellen and the white passengers sat inside. About seven miles from Halifax, the coach jerked to a stop. A wheel had come off. William was thrown on top of the driver, and was rather pleased that the prejudiced fellow was deeper in the mud than he was. The passengers, who had to proceed on foot, arrived in Halifax bruised, wet, and muddy. The coach arrived a few hours later with the luggage.

When the Crafts left Boston, they thought they would arrive in Halifax at least two or three days before the steamer from Boston. But the delays at Portland and St. Johns caused them to arrive two hours after the steamer had sailed for England. The next steamer, the *Cambria*, would not arrive for another two weeks.

The only good hotel in Halifax was closed, and the passengers had to stay in a miserable inn near the mar-

ket. Having become acquainted with Canadian prejudice in St. Johns, William asked Ellen to go in with the other passengers to engage a room for herself and her husband. William stayed downstairs and waited for the luggage.

The proprietress of the inn, noticing his interest in the luggage, went up to Ellen, and said, "Do you know the dark man downstairs?"

"Yes," Ellen answered. "He's my husband."

"No, I mean the black man—"

"I quite understand you. He's my husband."

The landlady flounced out.

A little later, Ellen ordered tea. The word came back that they must take it in the kitchen or in the bedroom. They could not be served with the other guests.

The next morning the landlady came up, and asked how long they expected to stay.

"We plan to stay two weeks, until the steamer *Cambria* comes," William answered.

"I am sorry, but we shall not be able to accommodate you," said the landlady. "Please understand that I myself do not object to having you here. I feel nothing but friendship for colored people. But the guests—they won't hear of it nohow. They would all have left last night if there had been anywhere else to go. I cannot afford to lose all my customers."

"We have no wish to offend your guests or spoil your business," William answered. "If you will find us suitable accommodations we shall be glad to leave." (He thought to himself that it wouldn't be hard to find a better place than this run-down, shabby inn where they were not wanted.)

After spending an entire morning looking for other accommodations for them, the landlady came back to say that she had been unsuccessful. "Perhaps," she suggested, "a family of your race would take you in under the circumstances," and she gave William the names of some families.

The first man William called on, the Reverend Mr. Canady, said he and his wife would be glad to have the Crafts stay with them. When William insisted on paying for room and board, Mr. Canady would accept only a small amount.

Despite the kindness of the Canadys, the Crafts' stay in Halifax was not a pleasant one. They were both ill, having been not well when they left Boston, and then taking cold on the journey to Halifax. In addition, they had difficulty getting tickets for the trip to London. At the office of the Cunard Line the ticket agent said that they did not book passage until the steamer came, which was not true. When William came again, he was told that the *Cambria* would come full from Boston, and there would be no room for them. He was advised to find some other way of getting to Liverpool. Fortunately Francis Jackson, a Boston abolitionist and member of the Vigilance Committee, had given William a letter of introduction to a friend in Halifax. He turned out to be a man of some prominence, who rebuked the representatives of the Cunard Line for their attitude and actions, and helped William get the needed tickets for the voyage to England.

Ellen was quite ill when they boarded the *Cambria*. During the voyage her heavy cold developed into pneumonia. One terrible night Ellen was so weakened by fever that William thought she would not live until morning. Had they dared so much and come so far to have her life and their dreams end here at sea? William held her hand as he prayed that she might live to step on the free soil of England. Toward morning the fever broke.

When the *Cambria* landed at Liverpool a few days later, Ellen, pale and weak, was sufficiently recovered to leave the ship, leaning on William's arm.

They arrived in England just two years after their escape from Georgia.

In Liverpool the Reverend Francis Bishop and his wife invited the Crafts to stay with them. Under their care, Ellen slowly recovered her health. While there, William sent Mr. Estlin the Reverend Samuel May's letter of introduction. Mr. Estlin immediately invited the Crafts to stay with him in Bristol.

When Ellen and William arrived, Mr. Estlin and his sister welcomed them so warmly that they were reminded of their first hosts, Mr. and Mrs. Barkley Ivens, the Pennsylvania Quakers.

It was not long before the Crafts met another fugitive slave then visiting England—William Wells Brown. Like Ellen, Brown was the child of his master and a slave mother. A bright, strong youth, he had found slavery intolerable, and had made a daring escape when he was eighteen years old. He had not kept his slave name, but had added the name of *Wells Brown*, a Quaker who had helped him, to his own first name, *William*.

In the North, William Wells Brown had become a steward on a Lake Erie steamer. In the course of one year he had given free passage to Canada to sixty-five fugitive slaves. Although William had never had a day of schooling, he taught himself to read and write, and achieved such proficiency that he later became a novelist and playwright. He was also an eloquent public speaker, using his talents to promote two causes—world peace and the abolition of slavery.

In 1849 the American Peace Society elected William Wells Brown a delegate to a conference on peace to be held in Paris. When the conference ended, he went to England where he stayed for five years. There Ellen and William Craft joined him in a tour of England and Scotland, meeting many prominent people—clergymen, statesmen, and authors—and speaking at anti-slavery meetings.

William Wells Brown later wrote a book called *The American Fugitive in Europe: Sketches of Places and People Abroad* telling the story of his travels and describing how warmly people reacted to the story of the Crafts. One of the prominent people they visited was Miss Harriet Martineau, author of *Society in America*, a social reformer and feminist, who had almost been mobbed in the United States because of her abolitionist views.

Miss Martineau, whom the Crafts visited at her home in England's Lake Country, wept as she listened to William Craft's recital of his and Ellen's story. Then she exclaimed, "I would that every woman in the British Empire could hear that tale as I have, so that they might know how their sex was treated in that boasted land of liberty."

After the Crafts returned to Bristol, they appeared with William Wells Brown at a great anti-slavery meeting held in that city on April 9, 1851. Ten days later an article about the Crafts appeared in the *Illustrated London News*, with a picture of Ellen in the disguise in which she had escaped from the South.

In Bristol the Estlins arranged for William and Ellen Craft to continue their education at a school kept by two sisters, the Misses Lushington. There the headmaster took special interest in his capable but so far unschooled students, and Ellen and William made remarkable progress.

At this time Ellen Craft had an illustrious visitor in the small cottage in which she and William lived. When Lady Byron, the widow of the famous English poet, came to see Ellen, she entered a small, plainly furnished room. On the table she saw copies of the *Liberator* and *Frederick Douglass's Paper*. Ellen was sitting near the window, busily sewing, with a spelling-book lying open in her lap, so absorbed in her work that a few minutes passed before she looked up. Then Lady Byron and Ellen Craft talked for more than an hour; Lady Byron's eyes filled with tears as Ellen described her life as a slave and her experiences as a fugitive.

Ellen and William Craft, William Wells Brown, and their English friends were determined to take advantage of every opportunity to sway public opinion in England and the world against slavery. A unique event was scheduled to take place in London, an event which would attract visitors from all over the world—the Great Exhibition at the Crystal Palace. Under the sponsorship of Prince Albert, this was the first international exhibition of the products of industry ever held—the forerunner of all the world's fairs and international expositions which have been held periodically ever since.

Prince Albert opened the Great Exhibition on May 1, 1851. The tremendous building was filled with exhibits from all over the world. Visitors, too, came from all over the world. As many as 64,000 people came in a single day, yet the Crystal Palace did not seem overcrowded.

What an opportunity this would be to present the evils of slavery before the world! But there was no chance for a meeting, or a speech, or an exhibit.

In the American exhibit there was a famous statue —"The Greek Slave" by Hiram Powers. The British humorous magazine *Punch* had published a cartoon, in imitation of that statue, which it captioned "The Virginia Slave." It was suggested that the Crafts and William Wells Brown attend the exhibition and stand in front of the statue of "The Greek Slave" holding the *Punch* cartoon. They would be a living exhibit of American slavery. Sixteen friends accompanied William Wells Brown and the Crafts to the Crystal Palace, and left them standing in front of "The Greek Slave," in the hope that passersby would question them. Throngs of people looked, stared, and walked on. The fugitives stayed at their post for six or seven hours, without engaging anyone in discussion. They finally went home, disappointed. But William Craft came again another day and that day did manage to get a few Americans to argue the merits of slavery with him.

A few months later, on August 1, 1851, the fugitives were at the Hall of Commerce at a tremendous antislavery meeting chaired by William Wells Brown. They celebrated the anniversary of West Indian emancipation, which had taken place in August, 1834, and reminded those present that slavery still existed in the United States, and that here were some of its victims to testify to its cruelties. Many distinguished Englishmen attended the meeting, among them the poet and historian Thomas Babington Macauley and the poet Alfred, Lord Tennyson.

Ellen and William had not been in England long before William was able to get a good job. Now, with a job, a place to live, and freedom, they were ready to have a family. They raised four sons—Charles Phillips, William, Braum, and Alfred—and a daughter, Ellen.

Throughout their years in England, Ellen and William did not forget their family and friends, and all those who still suffered in slavery. William had never stopped trying to find his parents and his brothers and sister who had been sold before he was put on the auction block, and the sister who had been auctioned at the same time he was. He finally found out where his mother was and purchased her from her owner. His mother then tried to locate her daughter and finally traced her to a family in Mississippi. With money William earned and with the help of English friends, he succeeded in purchasing his sister's freedom, enabling her to be reunited with their mother. His silent prayer at the time of the slave auction was answered at last!

In 1859 Theodore Parker, who had been very ill, traveled to Europe in the hope of restoring his health. In London he had a special visitor—Ellen Craft. They reminisced about old times, about the flight to the Lorings' house, the wedding, and all the other adventures in Boston. Since the Crafts' escape, Parker said, Boston had been the refuge of other fugitive slaves who had been captured by Southern agents. Some, like Shadrach, had been boldly rescued; others, like Sims and Anthony Burns, had been taken back into slavery in spite of all the efforts of the Vigilance Committee. Mr. Parker was happy to see that at least these two of the fugitives who had been his parishioners were safe, well, and happy.

In the years that followed, William and Ellen read of the events of the Civil War with great interest, sympathizing with their people. In 1865, when a draft call caused riots in New York City, and an orphanage for black children was burned down, Ellen sent the children bundles of clothing she had sewed for them.

A comfortable house, the esteem of those who knew them, children, work, freedom . . . England spelled all these. Yet William and Ellen knew they were far from home.

IX

Home Free

When the Civil War was over, the slaves freed, and the United States united once more, William and Ellen Craft began to long for their old home. They talked to their children about going back—their English children, who had been born and educated in England and who knew no other home. Their son William decided to remain in England, but the others agreed to go back to the United States.

William and Ellen had saved a good deal of money in England, and knew that they would be able to establish themselves in their native country.

Where to settle? The Crafts visited their old friends in Boston and New York. Rev. John Chadwick, a friend of Theodore Parker, invited William to speak in his church in Brooklyn. But the place which drew them back was Georgia, where they could now purchase land and live in freedom. They bought a plantation of 1,800 acres in Bryan County, Georgia.

But Ellen and William Craft could not live in comfort when their people needed them. True, Negroes were no longer slaves, but they were still in chains of poverty and ignorance. Although schools for black children had been established in the cities and large towns of Georgia, children who lived in the country were still not able to get an education.

William and Ellen therefore established the Woodville Cooperative Farm School on their land, inviting poor families to live there, share their work, and send their children to the school. William consulted with his friends in Boston and New York about how to run the school and received gifts of books from publishers, such as Harper Brothers, and from individuals.

Ellen and their sons taught the children, receiving very little payment.

Now William and Ellen were poor again, having put all their money into the plantation and even taking a mortgage of $2,500 in order to restore some old buildings on the land and build new houses and a schoolhouse, which also served as a church.

In 1875 William wrote a letter to the *Boston Daily Advertiser* describing the cooperative, and saying proudly:

> There are seventy-five boys and girls on our books, most of whom attend regularly. Thirty pupils reside here, the others come from the neighborhood free. Eighteen months ago only eight or ten of the children that now attend the school knew the alphabet, but now most of them can read and write quite intelligibly. . . .

* * *

William and Ellen spent the rest of their lives on the plantation in Georgia. Their children and grandchildren

used to love to visit them there. One of their grandsons, Henry Kempton Craft (son of their son, Charles Phillips) remembers that every day when the train whose tracks cut across their property was due to come, Grandfather William stood on the porch to watch for it.

Did the train remind him of train rides of the past— of the escape to Baltimore, to Boston, to Canada?

Or did it remind him that trains take you away and home again?

Or, holding his little grandson's hand, did he foresee that his children and grandchildren, who had never been slaves, would still have to purchase their own tickets to freedom?

Sources

Two Tickets to Freedom is based largely on William Craft's narrative, *Running a Thousand Miles for Freedom*. This book, which was originally published in England in 1861, has been reprinted with an introduction by Florence B. Freedman (Arno Press and *The New York Times*, 1969). Other incidents in *Two Tickets to Freedom* are based on contemporary documents: newspaper articles about the Crafts and books written by people who knew the Crafts.

Information about the owners of William and Ellen when they were slaves comes from the researches of Father Albert Foley, S.J., Ph.D., of Spring Hill College, Mobile, Alabama.

The author learned about the Crafts' children and their later years in Georgia from Mr. Henry Kempton Craft of New York City, grandson of William and Ellen Craft.